Catholic
Priest

Julia Roche

Photographs by Chris Fairclough

W
FRANKLIN WATTS
LONDON•SYDNEY

First published in 2001 by
Franklin Watts
96 Leonard Street
London EC2A 4XD

Franklin Watts Australia
56 O'Riordan Street
Alexandria
NSW 2015

© 2001 Franklin Watts

ISBN 0 7496 4092 8

Dewey Decimal Classification Number 282

A CIP Catalogue record for this book is
available from the British Library

Series Editor: Ruth Nason
Design: Carole Binding

Reading Consultant: Lesley Clark, Reading
and Language Information Centre, University
of Reading

The Author and Publishers thank
Father Eugene J. Fitzpatrick and all the
people at Our Lady of Lourdes, Harpenden,
for their help in preparing this book.

Printed in Malaysia

Contents

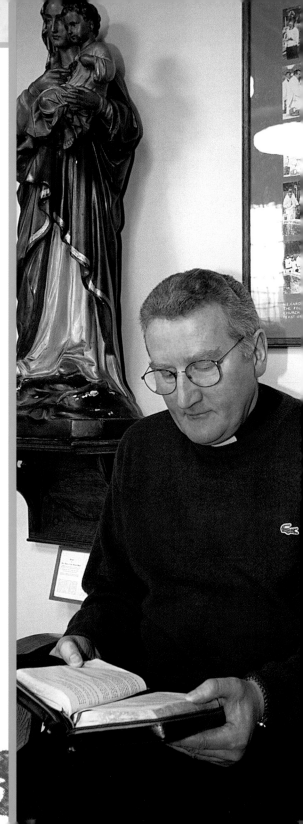

Hello!

I'm Father Eugene, a priest at a Catholic church in Harpenden, near London.

I lead services in the church. I teach people about Catholic beliefs, and I try to show how these beliefs can help people in their daily lives.

Catholics call their priests 'Father'. They trust the priest to be like a father, loving and caring for everyone – from the youngest to the oldest.

Mary and Jesus

Catholics believe that God chose Mary to be the mother of his son, Jesus. At Christmas we remember how Jesus was born in a stable in Bethlehem and we build a model of the stable in our church.

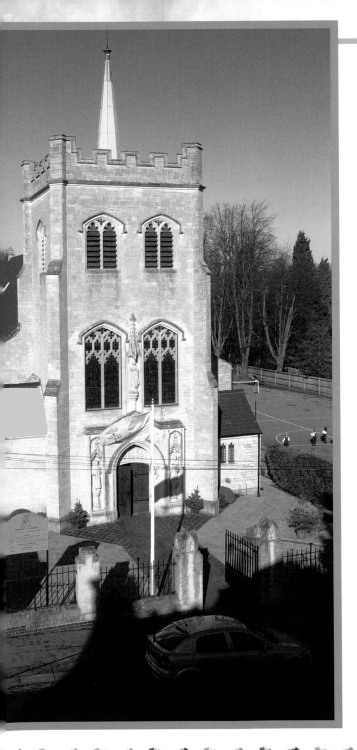

Our church is called Our Lady of Lourdes. Our Lady is another name for Mary.

Catholics honour Mary as the mother of Jesus. We have statues of her in our churches, in the same way that we have photographs of our families at home.

9

Mass

Mass is the most important service for Catholics. I say Mass in church every day, at a special table called an altar.

The clothes I wear for Mass are called vestments. I wear different coloured vestments at different times of the year.

During the first part of the Mass we listen to readings from the Bible. We believe this is one way in which God speaks to us.

Then members of the congregation carry gifts of bread and wine to the altar. This part of the Mass is called the Offertory.

Communion

The main part of the Mass is about sharing a meal, as Jesus did with his apostles.

I perfume the bread and wine with incense, and I bless them and pray over them. Then I say the words that Jesus said:

'Take this, all of you, and eat it: this is my body which will be given up for you.'

Catholics believe that, at this moment, Jesus becomes truly present, in the form of wine and the small round wafer of bread called the host.

Now we share the meal, which we call Holy Communion.

After the meal I clean the special cups that we have used.

Helping at Mass

Each weekend young people come to be servers at Mass. Servers prepare the altar, light the candles and bring me the things I need. Before the Mass, I talk to them about what they will be doing.

Other young people come to sing in the choir. The servers wear white and the choir wear blue. We all pray together before going into the church.

Family Mass

There are always lots of children at our family Mass on Sunday. Some of them do the Bible readings and carry the gifts in the Offertory procession.

I speak to the children and their parents about Jesus and how he wants us to be loving and praying people. The children and I share ideas about the stories Jesus told.

After Mass, I enjoy talking to people as they come out of church.

Visiting the sick

An important part of my work is to visit people when they are sick.

Before I go, I take a host from the tabernacle, so that I can give Holy Communion to the ill person.

At the person's home, I talk to them, give them Communion and pray with them.

Sometimes, if a person is very ill, I give them an extra blessing and put some holy oil on them. This is called the Sacrament of the Sick.

Sacraments

For Catholics, the sacraments are like meetings with Jesus at special times in our lives.

A new baby receives the sacrament of Baptism.

When two people love each other and want to spend the rest of their lives together, they receive the sacrament of Marriage.

Sometimes a person wants to say sorry or ask God for help to do better. Then he or she receives the sacrament of Reconciliation.

I listen to what the person says and we give thanks for all the good things that have happened. I then give the person a blessing as a sign of God's forgiveness.

The parish family

Catholics in the parish, or neighbourhood, around our church are like one big family. We come together to pray, to have fun, and to work for people all over the world who need our help. The notices tell people about our work.

One special time for prayer is Advent, the four weeks before Christmas. Each Sunday we light one more candle on the Advent wreath to remind us that Jesus's birthday is coming.

Last year we had a Christmas tree festival in the church. The festival raised money for sick children who need special care.

Out and about

I am a governor at the Catholic school in the parish, so I have meetings with the head teacher.

Sometimes I visit the Toddlers' Group. I watch the children play and I chat with their mums and dads.

I also go into school to see the children. We share our news about events at home, in school and at church.

Talking and praying

Talking is the best way of getting to know people, so I am glad when people come to talk to me. Sometimes people come because they are worried or need advice, and I try to help them.

I like to share ideas with ministers from other churches. I also like to invite people for a meal, so that we can talk and get to know each other more. Catholic priests do not marry, so I live on my own. I enjoy cooking!

Talking to God is also the best way of getting to know him, and therefore I like to start and finish my day in prayer.

Glossary

apostles
The twelve special friends of Jesus, who helped to spread his good news of God's love.

Baptism
The first of the seven sacraments, by which children or adults become members of God's family.

Bible
The Christian holy book.

blessing
A special prayer; saying a special prayer over something.

Christmas
The 12 days from 25 December (Christmas Day) when Christians celebrate the birth of Jesus Christ.

church
A building where Christians meet to pray and worship God.

congregation
All the people who are attending a service.

governor
A person who, with several others, is responsible for the running of a school.

Holy Communion
One of the seven sacraments, at which Catholics receive Jesus in the form of a wafer of bread.

honour
To consider or treat with special respect.

incense

A substance which gives off a sweet smell when it is burned. It is burned in a special container and is used as a sign of respect.

Jesus

A man who lived and died in Palestine 2,000 years ago. Christians believe that Jesus was the son of God and came back to life on Easter Sunday.

Lourdes

A place in the south of France where Our Lady appeared to a girl called Bernadette.

prayer

The way in which people talk to God.

sacrament

For Catholics, a sacrament is a visible sign of a meeting of their hearts and minds with Jesus, at special times in their lives. There are seven sacraments: Baptism, Holy Communion, Reconciliation, Confirmation (to mark a person's growing up in their faith), Marriage, the Sacrament of the Sick and Holy Orders (to make someone a priest).

services

Occasions when people meet in church to pray.

tabernacle

A beautifully decorated, locking cupboard above the altar, where the hosts are kept.

Index